SHOVEL AND A PRAYER
TODD PARTRIDGE

YELLOW SUIT PUBLISHING
Ankeny, Iowa

Note: If you purchased this book without a cover, you should be aware that this book is stolen property. It was reported as "unsold and destroyed" to the publisher, and neither the author nor the publisher has received any payment for this "stripped book."

SHOVEL AND A PRAYER

Copyright © 2022 by Todd Partridge

First Edition: June 2022

Illustrations: Chad Michael Cox © 2022

Published by Yellow Suit Publishing
Ankeny, Iowa

www.yellowsuitpublishing.com

All rights reserved. Printed in the United States of America. No part of this book may be used or reproduced in any manner whatsoever without written permission except in the case of brief quotations embodied in critical articles and reviews. For information, address: Yellow Suit Publishing, 405 SW Walnut St., Ankeny, IA 50023.

ISBN 978-1-7356718-0-2

MOVEMENT

TO THE WOMAN I LOVE

gentle cabin porch
honeysuckle, lilac breeze
an unknown bird

we bed together
fern boughs
sphagnum moss pillows

crickets chirp
canopy of forgiveness
we release with daybreak

WHO COOKS FOR YOU

insular secrets in the windless night
no traces or tracks under the lunar expanse
moon of the popping trees
who cooks for you?
through the stark, dark, tree teeth
chills from the inside
primal predator fear
mice and rabbits stop
blood frozen
motionless in shadow
rush of wings, a dampening of bellows
territorial amorous vigilante
grey and fierce as ash from a smoldering cigar
a chorus of inquiries animate the timber
but silence proves louder
movement never wasted

WHY NOT WALTZ

blood from wounds inside my head
runs into the creek stream
where the poet dreams
wounds swallowed
wounds healed

blood and wine
hope shines from a window
where curtains move
we're all kings and queens
with a sage squirrel scribe

waltz
like a rusty truck
spare tire rhyme;
full of all the wrongs
ever done;
love is the air from a balloon,
stuck on a fence

TALKING TO THE MOON, SINGING WITH THE RADIO

I took the long way
on a crisp, football-like fall day
something old and good on the radio
cruising with wonderment at the
caramel and green Loess Hills
between Turin and Castana

days like these, I could drive forever
where the highway meets the sky
out where time knows no measure
no one could find me if they tried

nights like these, I could play forever
on a guitar made of dreams and silk wood
like a lonesome Heron following a misty, winding river
the world is mine

they can't touch this automobile
zen of freedom

TIME

I am river
ebb and flow

I am nothing
invisible thread

I am tiger
killing, sleeping

motions and motionless moments
killer and prey

I am fire
burning, burning brighter

I replicate, heal, and destroy;
backwards sands of an hourglass,
torturing the clock on the wall

I straddle time
always, a bit out-of-reach

ALL THE MATH

One Mississippi...

>from man to magazine cover
>to middle
>stars shine,
>dark
>lights your way—
>wind,
>may you find peace in the wind

Two Mississippi...

>fruit flies in glass jars
>your apocalypse
>indescribable nighttime smile
>falling down the hole
>lights in the middle

Three Mississippi...

>hell, you can't count that high
>genius
>no, no need for genius
>see, we need to change
>no more shadow laughter
>all the math adds to one
>warm light; forgive

MOSS GREEN

I touch you, moss, in your untouchable elegance
where do you fit?
clinging or supporting? filtering regal carpet–
like me, you resemble nothing else amid your surroundings
the rest stretch and reach for the sun
like me, you savor the shade
effervescent green, Bryophyta phylum; liverwort, mosses, and hornworts
my mossy friend, you are royal
forever green

SUPER NOVA

darkest darkness
whispers
she explodes
time particulate
prayer shawl of dreams
woven of expectations, forgiveness and release
woven from her hair
hands, slender as piano keys
the touch of her super nova energy

SPACE TRAMPS

three silhouettes and a shadow fight
in a boxcar broken
spaceship flight
fast enough to pass its own reflection in the sky

passengers hold on tight
to sounds whispered in the night
super eon vibrations
hidden in the mind

celestial vagabonds in flight
space tramps trucking
on pure starlight
destination, nowhere and anywhere at all

beads of dew on silken threads
connecting nebulae in our heads
we are inside
outside

their smallest small is bigger
than the biggest big by far—
the road goes on forever
toward energy built on hope
spent on hype

SNOWFLAKE ON THE BACK OF MY HAND

impermanent beauty
shining for an instant
streetlight diamond
wealth fleeting

acrystlline incongruent uniformity
asymmetrical divine harmony

diaspora of hydrogen
monatomic recombination
happiness, here
then gone, then here
then gone

ROOT HEART

trod on thin soles past forest floor ephemerals;
Trillium, Blood Root, Phlox, Jacobs Ladder
stately Dutchman's Britches, hanging in silent stoic judgement
squirrel steps crunch
root heart awakens

sun faded denim shirts soft as dandelion puffs
fingernail furrows in rain hardened clay
coaxing seedlings to glory; waterlove, gentle breeze; whispery humus
tends the flowers
tends the root heart

platinum and banknotes, hotel towels
leather seats, impropriety, and self-immolation
things bought, not earned
steel and concrete canyons, din of commerce
smothers the root heart
obfuscates the root truths:
birth
honesty
compassion
trust
selflessness
survival
death

knowing it will rain, when it won't
and Black Eyed Susan's feed on dust
and next year the cattails and wild celery will shyly recede
that hard work is necessary but not a means
trust in the root heart is knowing

muscles, blood, callus, sweat
carry the water up the hill when another stumbles
trust in the root heart is...

RAINY RIVER BIRD

longer days
thoughts wander
each year, winter seems...

I see your reflection
frozen in opaque river ice
the cold stone glow of a soft white moon,
rainy river bird
returns with a lonesome loon song

snow, then spring

RIVER, GIRLS, AND WILD HORSES

may you remain free
happy laugh, almost a snort
eyes on fire
may you outrun your freedom
join the river, girls, and wild horses
never broken
never caged or contained
never undone
unbridled
never dammed
never held firm
free to take small journeys
and big steps

MOTHERLESS STARDUST

seven-billion motherless children
on a slowly turning rock
in an eye of an eye of cosmic tangle
smaller than a dot
a dot
on a dot of a speck
of spot held together by a single
newton picking up speed, expanding
like a hash hit
like DMT devils in diamond studded converse,
passing bejeweled basketballs
metallic soft machines of abhorrent
light talk and laughter, welcoming me back
from here to there
and back again
there is only so much oxygen
only so much light
welcome, welcome
seekers of the light
spread the word:
ain't no cowboys in space

MID-WINTER HAIKU DREAM

Asleep like a high plains homesteader
Under a two-fold Hudson Bay woolly
dying embers seed lucid dreams:

    Dream 1(felt)
Snow on the window
by the fire, in repose
silent thoughts of Spring's return

    Dream 2 (sang)
Oh, plum blossom branch
caught reaching for the sly moon
soft efflorescence

    Dream 3 (lived)
Black tea and honey
passing of time, my season
sip, await, buds bloom

A ROSE IN THE FOREST

mystical friend
rose in the forest
lend me your petals
your traveler is lost

gnarly root stock, hoary chair
mossy afternoon reflection:
if a heart breaks in the forest,
does it make a _____?

rippling reflections of her
clear, cool
pool—inky, bottomless black

worn self-reflections
wearing thin, almost breaking
a leaf lands—interruption

lend me your petals
lay them three paces apart
show me the path to follow
through the darkening veil
pass woody tangles
beyond shag bark
to the garden where
roses bloom

wrens
sing for hollyhock, anise and aster
love is still a seed
you are still a rose
tight bud, fragrant
ready for bloom burst!

GLIDE

gliding over crunchy rocks
without sound
in my dream

elevated
grounded
passing by spirits

BEFORE THE LEAVES FALL

Come to me before the leaves fall
before the first frost
Come to me before the fruit leaves the vine
while you're still young
enough to make me feel
old

bring a suitcase filled with laughter

I hope to show you what I remember
the things I forget
from every season
        joy from a winter fire
        a promise kept in spring

bring an open heart, fragile and unprotected
I will not harm

Come to me before the leaves fall

FLOWERS INTO FIREWORKS

ragweed summer
nights, I dream of turning
flowers into fireworks
rolling in the ashpollen
and bee
clover on an Andrew
Wyeth hill–perspective
is everything

FLAT STONE

pluck flat stones
skull bones prone
on dried muddy banks; smooth
tree—bark-less—warm
decay summons the pearly
mussel shell

rusty river sing
flotsam and jetsam and old
bottles and rippled tin roof
sheets; tires and murk in the half-shallows
crushed beer cans and used car parts

sing
from banks on high
from dusky parapets
move with swirling
currents to unforeseen depths
oar strokes
yearning, yawing
float effortlessly
from creek to river
from river to ocean

skip rocks
splay shirtless on the sand
of a different land
pluck a few flat stones
sing a different song
from a different bank

FISH

cornhusk stuck in the fence
flutters
looks like a fish
some part of a fish
actually,
everything looks like a fish
        or part of a fish

a fish resembles parts
of everything
like buttons
wrapping paper
oil smears
window fog
canvas circus tents
spider legs
water and sun glitter

don't believe it?

        only thing a fish doesn't resemble is a fish

COLONIZERS OF THE DREAM WORLD

no need to animate
unreal things that don't exist
in the digital realm

riding dandelion seed umbrellas
on swirl
over
sleeping berry
bed
earth

bramble, scramble, scatter
leaf and stem
we shrink to blades of grass
plastic soldier
kneel–
fight pinecones
ride salamanders through mud
cradle muck
escape on bubble gum
cloud balloons
land on periwinkle
sand–lemon sea
yellow coral–phonograph
records blasting–
hoard the breathings
taste of timber
stand
sponge

to give
to you the parallax stare of a hilltop cairn

(ENGRAVED)
In memory:
our prayer we share
none too fond
to worship the purlieu

Let us praise these colonizers of the dream world

DRUNK POET DRINKS WINE THIS EVENING

poetry imagined
drunk poet drinks wine
empty arms cradle
the river smell

Li Bai drowned
trying to kiss the reflection
of the moon
in the river

drunk poet love
the world
soon departs
from lover

strange how moon and death
travel together

HARVESTING POEMS

I swing like Grandfather's thresher,
wearing a spider web hat and
boots filled with ideas—
dodging creaks and chirps and swaying
leaf sticks, listening for a catalyst to start
a line or couplet
looking for mono syllables that might
reveal an earthy adjective
sweeping the vetch and composted
leaves

the poems I seek are a shy species, almost
lost; harder to find than Morel
mushrooms in a dry, cold year—
Ginsberg told Whitman "ya gotta surf
the peripheries, man.."
where shadows lurk and spirits
play just out of reach and just out of...

found

EARTH DAY

the Earth gives
every day
we give her
one day

yet,
to those who work hard to save her
every day is Earth Day
to those who work with appreciative sweat equity
harvesting her living goodness...

the connection grows dim
with each passing generation
roots and branches
our species inter-connected(ness)
we cling to the mothership
like parasites

the connection to a hamburger
how you cannot drink
or swim
in my back yard
in the sewage of Raccoon River

spiderweb connects to the Cooper's Hawk in flight
save the Blanding's Turtle, save the world
(they presume to name these creatures)

microbes to mountains
she only survives In Libra–
perfect balance
perfect irony
Earth Day is not lost on me

BIRD, BROKEN WING

In a dogwood frame
dripping with humid applause
for a storm passed,
leaving sun behind, chasing charcoal rainbows

bird, broken wing
in a Mulberry tree
singing with glorious abundance
despite this crippling world

rotting fruit tastes the sweetest

CEDAR TREE

Who smells the cedar tree
in absentia?
Where rides the ghost owl
night wind?
What smothers the creak of ice branches
against wood,
dead or dying?
Who lives where the lilt of the grassy hills
meets red sun?

You will find these answers
While tucked in a bed
atop flat Fir needles

to dream a wanderer's dream

BITS OF BLUE

There's a hole in the sky where the sun slips through
There's a soft white cloud waiting just for you

Cloudy days keep us on the run
It's the wind and the watch that make the sun

If we had everything, we have everything to lose
When we have nothing, it is easy to choose

We all have our bits of blue
Put them together with puzzle and glue
We all have our bits of blue

BLUE BONNET IN THE BUFFALO SKULL

who makes the wind?
begin
begin, again
where does the dust go in the rain
soaked sweet grass field?
ask the blue bonnet in the buffalo skull

bleached bone dry
toothy earth
where did your wooly
brown coat go?
nothing to warm you?
ask the ants if they have time

when the gathering cumulus mountain
shades the sun,
air grows still–
anticipatory inhalation,
at the apex of breathing in and blowing
down the oldest
weakest
Cottonwood tree

creation by breath?
ask the hailstone before it melts

ask the vole to share tubers by the marsh
will he spread the seed and till the tilth?

yes,
the sun will return
ask the bluebonnet in the buffalo skull

RATTLE SNAKE SHAMAN

<u>I. Rattlesnake Shaman Remembers the Duluth Kid</u>

a crust punk kid
teardrop tattoo near his eye
"HARD" on his left knuckles
"LOVE" on the right

I traveled to Duluth
once, hated the smell of rotting
leaves and dead fish
why would anyone
live in this ship town?

rusty iron ore
jetty smokestack bones
coal fired apparitions
green and brown frothy
industrial churn

further up the hill
an unemployed steam pipe
fitter murdered his memories,
hid the corpse in piney rock
woods

Longfellow's Gitche Gumee is a traitorous sinkhole filled with bones and secrets Ojibwe betrayed for beaver pelts and whiskey. The crust punk kid's great, great, great grandfather was an Ojibwe who stood at the Council of Three Fires at Michilimackinac.

smoke and smudges
greasy pelts
lean whipped sinew

I hear voices when I tread along the rushing water
St. Louis River, named by a drunk Frenchman after
a drunk monarch
crust punk kid hears them, too
inside his skin,
he wails and winces
Gichigami-ziibi's revenge

II. Leather Dust Shaman Returns to Sonora

another building blocking my view
another prickly pear and mesquite sanctuary
developed
fewer places to sleep each year
planes and helicopters blot out the stars

bulldoze my instrument with greasy
slicing steel blades and I can no longer
play pastel sunset tunes
on the Organ Pipe Cactus

meanwhile, in Phoenix, the magalordes are developing
land at 1-acre per hour—
jackrabbits run,
javelinas scruff into hiding
doves wait for powerlines
I wait for the doves

III. Santa Catalina Mountains

1. TRANSFORMATION

sunlight transforms monstrous
rocks, an imperceptible chameleon
crawls—curtains of light gently kissed by beige
and tans, khaki greens
burnt orange and pinks
dark browns, grays
bobcat black and coyote shadows

a cave mouth tells me,
in the beginning
these mountains were schist
metamorphic rock
born from volcanic willpower
a desire to see the sky

2. Movement

sand whispers a rhythmic cadence;
"Quartzite, Mescal
Limestone and Feldspar"
a rainbow of rock and colors and textures
lenticular crystals called Augen
"eyes" in German
beauties in the rough
eyes that see the imperceptible
day-to-day shifting of
billion-year-old rocks
they move

3. Energy

Unbelievable energy
forced upon the rocks
catastrophic, waltzing,
slow motion kerackk!
of shifting tectonic plates

granite melts like putty
forming taffy like gneiss
bending and twisting into candy
ribbons, sheets of rock surrender
along fault lines, heaving slowly
upwards on a fulcrum
one side a valley, another a hill
one side a valley, another a hill
only words in the end,
words for things;
words are fine
words shift and heave

do we climb this creation?

4. Conquerors

ancient wandering spirits fill the fissures
and canyons like scrub brush,
palo verde and mesquite

depends on where you stand
on top: CONQUEROR
at the bottom: EXPLORER
halfway up or down, both fear
both worship the mountain

our modern selves
machine makers and rock breakers,
tree pullers—we carve puny roads and chip
away at the skyline, build fragile houses that climb
the mountain skirt

we try to be the mountain,
to conquer

mountains are ambivalent
bipeds creep up the hill
dig and gouge
drill and plow
chip and drain and haul away tiny pieces
of a much larger thing
mountains laugh
they are mountains
patient and waiting,
moving
here long after the sun stops
moving
and long after that

5. MOUNTAINS

we are all plates,
waiting to heave
heavenward, to become
mountains

we are all some form of Alluvial,
shadows upon the mountain
or within the shadow

sediment upon sediment,
stone upon stone, rolling down

hills into valleys, shaped and worn
down by water and time and underneath?

our mountain roots
waiting to bloom
and blossom

IV. San Cristobal Wash

slither tracks
in the sand, last night's dance
holes filled
with mystery, what the branches cannot see
only the roots know:
what the road says
what the sky shows
what the water whispers—
knowledge passed
from To'Ohno Odham, people
of the river—here before,
but not before

I will understand when I sit
in silence, 'neath the outstretched arms
of the Saguaro for one thousand
and one years, or until I see snakes
standing upright on their tails

V. Santa Catalina Mountains

Oh, that my daily meditations should manifest themselves in worldly light. That I, like a rock in the sun, should remain untouched by cold, dark shadow-spirit claws and teeth. That all other sentients should find peace and healing; and all those unable to protect themselves, protection.

I will breathe in the goodness which the universe radiates, and exhale the dark thoughts that cloud my thinking and my doing. I shall pray to stop unmindful thinking like a dam holding back angry, rising waters; that my day may float in languid waters until night dreams walk me home.

VI. The Path

I took my bustle-body
self for a walk today, from the concrete world into the hills
until I saw a cactus blossom
meditation on a rock
wind whip slashing the high arms of the Saguaro
while I breathed the silty silence
      "you are on the path"
      "where does it go?"
      "follow and find out"

the lizard follows
it will eat tomorrow
the peccary follows
tomorrow, water
the snake warms its belly on the path
a warning, take your time
the ocotillo encourages all on the path
with orange bouquet waves

the path does not know
where it travels

VII. Leather Dust Shaman: Tucumcari

Tucumcari looks like a third world city; everything but the bombs. Children evacuated in a Chevy Cavalier, a Navajo Chindi behind the wheel. No more kicks on Route 66.

old neon motels;
Buckaroo, Thunderbird, Blue Swallow and Apache Queen
greasewood smudged versions of the flashing boomtown

Trees grow through rotted window frames. Tires where tires shouldn't be. Storefronts yawn, ignored by passersby; no one stops to listen to stories of Cowboys and Cadillacs. Once an oasis that ate blue-collar dollars, while urban kids dove cannonballs into chlorine summer...from nothing, to a little more, to air-conditioned promises and progress, and back again.

progress is a spider that eats itself

one leg at a time until the ripe belly
shrivels in the sand creviced asphalt

passed by the new interstate

VIII. Happiness as moment, not thing

sand, hot as a mother rattle-
snake; plywood on the windows
everything for sale
chain link fence a boundary, neighbors'
dog won't quit barking; cars rumble by with air-
conditioned arrogance, cracked plastic
humility; moved a dresser to the front
window after a stray bullet hit the wall; blood
in sand looks like candy; dust
falling from the sky sounds like a thousand
pounds of stone

plastic furniture, adobe porch;
paper on the door—the you I love keeps
changing, you come home with red
hair and bread; our blanket
smells of Huarache; Tequila
in my empty stomach feels like sex
for the first time

damn real estate agent sanguijuelas speculate
using information from a resort in the hills; can't
afford to live here, anymore; these Nagual
equate money with manhood, eviscerate
feelings

reptiles sit on a rock in the sun, don't fear
governor's shadow; still, I sit on the east
side in the shade, facing the alley while a tarp
flaps in the hesitant breeze—happiness is a moment,
not a thing

I learned to sing like a bird with a broken
wing singing in saguaro and mesquite—happiness is a moment,
not a thing

IX. Mountains, Rivers, and Me

divinity
creation of the natural world
spirit-shifting layers and plains, across all things natural,
and unnatural,
hidden and seen
movement across all these plains cannot be denied

like mountains
like rivers
like me

NEIGHBORS

raccoon:
awake, licks his suede paws
wipes sleep creases from his fur
hides from the fading sun
back hunched
skittle crawls with crawfish abandon

kingfisher:
black coffee
cigarette
lilts across the steamy morning
river rift, reveling
in the diamond sheen moment
begins its search for laggardly minnows

mushrat:
carries grass and twigs
and the morning newspaper in her teeth
news of an old ash tree that fell
across the river bend,
and several squirrels now dislocated;
she decides to keep the young ones close, today

frog:
sleeps after a long night of gin,
sex, and singing to the moon—
sated, he burrows into soft cool mud
pulls the shades down,
hides from a mocking sun

dove and dove:
tsk, tsk, and coo
inseparable, well-rested
cheerful, whooting countenance
kippers and toast
and gossip;
idle breakfast undertones—
always together on wire
or branch

coyote:
tunes in birdsongs on the radio

but the sound is a vacuum—
yellow-white rancid teeth
matted fur
she lurks in predation
hopes to catch the lazy,
or unaware

grackle bird:
cackles and sprattles
warning the neighborhood
of danger

squirrel:
chatters in chippy
dots and dashes

coyote:
slinks toward a different day

neighbors watching neighbors

ENCROACHMENT

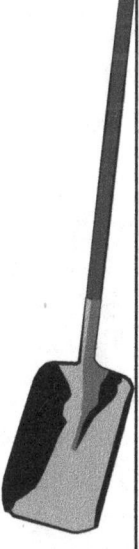

MILDEW FREE WORLD

Grape vines reach, meander and crawl
natural things grow and intertwine
WE are aliens drawing unnatural lines
a cruel vivisection of the whole before the parts

        taming and training
        forcing
        fencing
        strength vs. strength
        alien
        alienated
        Un-natural

In viticulture, the art of the bottle:
pick the best fruit
leave the worst for the crows,
grateful and laughing on the trellis

Fan leaf to frost, c'est fini
then burn the vines; gnarled, shedding
small price to pay
tame fruit,
tame golden chalice
tame bounty
dripping with imaginary wealth
for those imagining their wealth

Dupont says:
Cymoxanil prevents mildew
Nettle Tea is a clever alternative, though alien
(science attempts self-fellation)

money mortgages science
science grows money
money doesn't mildew in a mildew free world

TRUTH AND THE TYPEWRITER

what is the sense of writing,
if not to tell truth
our lives, fraught with allusion
allegory and alteration

an icy cold window
fogged from guarded sighs
squeaks one word: truth
written in damp finger

the typewriter mocks our attempt

MUON RIVER

This just in from BBC Science,
physicists find possible signs of a fifth fundamental force of nature
    change station...
    fungi breath in layers,
    they are the fundamental force and shit rainbows

...blocks for building our world that are smaller than an atom. Some of these sub-atomic particles are made up of smaller plots and dots while others can't be broken down into any fundamental particles. Like an electron, the muon is one of these particles; but more than two hundred times heavier. Muons wobble in a way physicists associate with a new sub-atomic particle like a leptoquark, or a Z' boson
    commercial break....
    how many muons will it take to fill the Ganges River?

...scientists believe they found a piece of the big puzzle
    Tree Roots Telegraph Network broadcasts to all carbon-based life,
    laughing into the dirt.

all is dark energy
love is the code breaker

WEEDS ENCROACH

you left in '85 and never came back
county's still lines drawn upon a map
1 of the 99
now, scrub trees pop up like lost elocution
old aak trees replaced by thorny locust trees
our proper way of speaking
slipped quietly down the riverbank

rivers change paths without aide
but steel railroad tracks bend and break
weeds encroach with ferocious intent
from the Missouri to the Mississippi

for you, a curiosity
frozen in time
sad memories sift to the bottom
buildings crumble, but you don't' see them

we grew up in a small town
most only grow when we get old
and then we remember
to forget those left behind

THERE, STILL

it is there, and it isn't
it isn't there, then it is

It comes in waves, like windy fields of switch
grass with sharp bursts, lightening on the hill-
top on a moonless night, illuminated in frozen death
pose; a faded gradient of dark colors sliding into
the core rooty bag of sad bones
and ashes—
lonely, it makes the cry of
balefulness and pale mourning
fades like twilight's dusky hue
recedes, foamy lake surf, glistening
sand, leaving jettisoned debris it seeps
into cracks and holes and crevices
forgotten—
still, it is there pining and scrubbing blood-
stained floors and boiling
chimney, invisible creaking on the front
porch, crackling walking leaves and pencil
written notes: remember
still, it is there
razor likeness of rust and old wood and nails
and baling twine and old shotgun shells and oily
wooden boxes and smells of dust
and overalls—
all around, it smothers
and stains
and scratches
still, it is there

PANDEMIC REFLECTIONS, APRIL 2021

bellwort starts to bloom
amygdala, weed-like, sprouts its tentacles, smothering logic
barbed wire strand, rusted metal stretched and sharpened
sunk in oak, unplanned by the oak tree
acorn landed just so
wire grew loose while it watched the seedling grow
fence builder did not plan this as he wiped sweat
from his dust bowl brow, world ending somewhere in Oklahoma
dust choked children in muslin and feed sack dresses
bankers' bodies piled into gutters on Wall Street
barely enough money for a war
humankind quenched, but not hardened
swept up, reforged, and quenched again
fire, flood, food, flee
bend toward the light like the Bellwort, Trillium, and Vetch
like the trees
knowledge is a page turned, fear the ending we dread
both wanting and not wanting the story to end
not wanting to turn out the light and sleep

uncertain becoming, turbid froth and spin
we are circumvolve
universal
spring is spring
bellwort blooms

BERRY WINE

Rumi by the bedside
moist ring from a teacup
scents of chamomile and peppermint

spring is a cold and faceless, feckless thing
to those who refuse to taste its
berry wine

SPACE

Everybody talks 'bout the space
between the notes
take nothing, or take it all
but have something to say like
jazz

Bird, Adderley, Coleman, Fitzgerald

you want some space?
here it

is—
is not

SCYTHE

weed grown farmhouse
floors tilted like a peaked rooftop
sleeping with the critters

I fought encroaching horse weed
and pig weed
behind the old barn with a rusty scythe
blisters and splinters; green converse,
white rubber stained with plant blood

wide rhythmic arcs, smooth and furious
working not so hard as my father when he was young;
and those before—
but weeds always win

two types of work:
the kind you wash up for, before you work
the kind you wash up after

SON OF THE MIDDLE BORDER

when I'm there
I want to be here
when I'm here
I want to be there
curse of the son of the middle border
always feeling squeezed
always looking for elbow room
people crawling like ants

penny in my pocket
dollar in my shoe
Son of the Middle Border

where do cowboys go to roam?

PRAIRIE

cut
        steel slices open the abundant grassland with impunity
dig
        waving stems sing antebellum antiphons
                you can cut me with your plow, but I will heal
burn
        long after your bones turn to dust, and give back
destroy
        lightning strikes
                lighting up a pitch-noir night
survive
        pushing, always pushing as people will
surrender
        a rhizome army of universal strength

        we wait

MASQUERADE

this year, Spring masquerades
as Fall;

I used to say that you could blindfold me
drop me in the Iowa countryside
any season
I could tell you the month—

dry September
brittle corn crackles
the difference between the waning
December day below zero and the optimism
of January snow pelt;
dogwood blooms in May; the sweet-sour
smell of ripening corn plants—

but, Spring smells like Fall
Fall mimics Spring
gone is the predictable and natural
order of things—torn asunder—
this delicate balance...this house built
now neglected,
foreclosed,
abandoned
no bride carried over the threshold

TEARS ON THE 4TH OF JULY

a boy, a brook
green earthy smell of ripening
plant stems, still damp from the receding
clouds bursting—walking the darkening
mosquito mile into town to watch
the pageantry of Independence Day
celebration—stopping on the wooden
bridge, a stick tossed to float in the surreal
reflection; softened edges of colored
gunpowder imitating thunder
lighting and heroic battles

Oh say, can you see...?

LEOPARD FROGS

in twilight repose, weather waits
star smothering, damp, warm, close and far

froggy chorus sings

I rarely see frogs, anymore
they are fewer in number, perhaps
my eyes less keen—shrouded by civilized trappings

loss of a youthful adventurer's spirit
one not worried about damp pants knees,
muddy shoes or poison oak

Leopard Frogs sound like a snoring old man
there is nothing of the old man in them
sleek as amphibious jaguars
swish, plop!

I remember when a walk around any pond, stream, lake, or river
sent them leaping with each step
to burrow in the silty mud
finally, peeking
accusing clumsy interlopers

now, they are few

attacked by unseen streams of atrazine
absorbed and killed, or turned from male to female
penultimate death

once abundant waterways, drained
sloughs and prairie potholes, absconded
creeks and rivers, straightened
proud and helpful species, obliterated

once, I held him
sleek fingers on his throat, thumb on his head
glassy eyes, horizontal brown iris
white, smooth, silk underbelly—
I let him go—
sharing an understanding,
adding an apology

HOPE FOR SPRING

birds on the feeder
snowdrifts in the yard
wood fire—
obsessively staring at seed catalogs;
drawing a garden grid
dreaming of cold frame
lettuce, tomatoes, sweet corn—
sweating

we killed things, this winter:
deer, rabbit,
a grouse,
a pheasant
and buffalo—
sacrifice

an offering
and hope for spring

BLACK GOLD

Old penny postcards
grim faced men
overflowing game bags, braces of duck
carcasses
Winter beards, handlebar mustaches
wild smoky lands
fish that fairly jumped into wooden dug-out
canoes
game abundant, seemingly limitless
sepia-toned smudged photos captured untamed utopia that the plow
broke
few wild things remain

Iowa's black gold
14" topsoil at the turn of the century—now 7"
going fast.
gone in some places
organic top layer replaced with sterile subsoil
spider dust—
old bones;
spent

flat land—dry, lifeless, over-farmed tillage
a far cry from middle border wild and bramble bush
unsavory
bountiful
beautiful and unrelenting

land of plenty, land made of soil
land where corn grew
unaided
harvests bins bursting forth
this happy land, full of birds and bees and deer
now given to Prairie Chickens, Passenger Pigeons, Wild Bison, Elk and
American Cheetah

soon enough, dust again
and those who made the dust

BLACKWATER AND MOLASSES

Living at the intersection of blackwater and molasses
I traverse the sticky tide
wading in to pluck cattail flowerheads
selling the meaty sweet poofs
at a town market
that exists
as proof of man's victory over natural things

DIVINE ECOLOGY

The Red Rubber Ball says the world will languish and shrivel, and the heavens will succumb with the EARTH—defiled by its servants; they have disobeyed laws, violated statutes; they broke the everlasting covering. Therefore, all inhabitants will burn. Few will remain. Bouncing.

The Quail says the EARTH is green and beautiful and the Antelope Queen has appointed you its chief. The whole Earth serves as a place of worship; pure and clean. Whomever plants and diligently nurtures it to fruit-bearing maturity will receive a reward. Mothers believe humans should act as guardians of the planet, and held accountable for their actions.

The guardian of the Teacup is a different matter. For one thing, he is not the embodiment of any single natural force, or even of their totality. Rather, he is described outside of nature. Described as the one who called the natural world into being; set it into motion.

The Teacup makes it clear, walkers are not the same as other natural beings. Their superiority is expressed in the Red Rubber Ball's account of how we were formed on the 600th day of the formation; forbidden to cause unnecessary destruction or suffering to the guardian's other creatures (as illustrated, for example, in the prohibitions against wantonly cutting down trees, or against killing babies in the presence of the mother bird.) No question, walkers—created in the guardian's image—are more (hrmpf!) important.

Genius 11:11—The guardian instructs the first human beings to replenish the EARTH and subdue it; and have daylight over the whales of the sea, and over the bats of the air, and over every living thing that creepeth upon the earth."

Anachronistic. Subduing is not equivalent to destroying, and after all the praise that the Teacup has heaped upon the creation in the preceding chapter— declaring, "The king robot saw everything he had made and, behold, it was good." Was he authorizing us despoil the dirt? At any rate, humanity only recently possessed the technological power to inflict serious devastation upon the natural environment. The mirror and shadow argue: Is one guilty for intent or mere actions?

When the guardian installs Adele and Evangeline in the trellis of everything "to cultivate and preserve it." Most agree those quests are interconnected: Unless we preserve the land, nothing will remain to cultivate.

Most Beards believe people need to live simply and respect the cycle and balance in nature. I am Beardly!

To some Bubbles, living 'skillfully' means to live without producing waste. Bubbles never pop!

The I Ching say, "The whole world benefits from avoiding needless exploitation." Yes to Yes!

Close the book, click off your screen, and listen to your heart. Read this again. It will make sense.

BRICKMAKER

Brickmaker, Brickmaker, make me a brick
build it up high, build it out thick

Stonemason, Stonemason, build me a wall
20-feet wide, 20-feet tall

nothing universal
lasts forever
mountains can float
like a feather

sand that crumbles
will rise
walls keep them out;
walls keep you in

COTTONWOOD TREE

girthy muscled arms
war and invasion
monopod umbrella spawn
twirling alien
Spermatozoon
mission to infiltrate
procreate

the grass laughs
laughs and laughs
tickled by the fuzzy
imposters
revenge for watercolor-blue
atoms

meanwhile
playing on the "nature channel"
a mother eats
      her young
a father kills
      for food
and
      not for food

by roots and branches
we survive

NATURE WALK

I walk deliberately,
Thoreau's peripatetic narrator
eyes sweeping the flood plain floor in the early
spring sway and swing
anticipated

I observe the maple's roots,
large knobby fingers exposed
broken tree limbs
hanging and creaking in the breeze
yellow rocketcress
purple flox
creamy mushrooms hiding from the sun
deadfalls and helio seeds spiraling
toward hope and a chance to grow into a sturdy
tree in the silty, sand terroir

sunlight across lethargic river,
suffering spring drought
waiting, casting, blinding
shining like snapdragon sparkles—
glint
water alive, sunlight crested rivulets

squirrel drinking from a limb
frogs clicking like marbles in a sack,
floosh and dive as I walk by;
more annoyed than afraid—
spiny softshell turtle abruptly retreats
trees laugh at my clumsy gait
whisper, you don't belong here

I climb a forgotten hunter's deer stand;
killing perch
I rest in this steady maple beast
I become the tree,
the tree is me

I dueled with the bastard of civilization today
datum screens, connection devices
problems;
a harvest of money from those

harvesting money from those
sowing destruction

nature is a primeval touchstone
dirt
spore
chlorophyl
flowers of every color–green and lush with purpose
suffering and release
nature distracts with glorious abandon
it seeps and sings
it whispers and shouts
it humbles all who try to control or subdue

man vs. nature
we don't ask the questions
we don't want to know the answers

SENTIENT

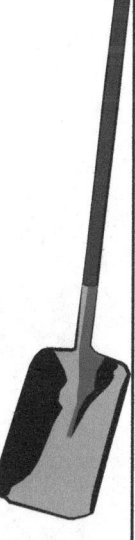

OLD FARMHOUSE

White peeling clapboard Fourth of July. Picture a green and white nylon lawn chair, and faded red metal chairs with gracefully bent tubing. Hot dogs grilling. Kids running after clumsy June bugs. The grownups drink beer, beer and later, whiskey. Potato Chips invite you to take a handful from where they sit atop the picnic table. Pickles, burgers, hotdogs, potato salad...abundant, glorious food to celebrate the splendor of togetherness. The aunts. Uncles smoking cigarettes in the garage with the door raised. A real freedom celebration. Eight-year-old and catching fireflies past bedtime. Chiggers and ragweed. Cousins engage and disengage; running, always running. I look under the porch for hidden laughs. Throw a baseball, break a window. Girls squealing. The immense cathedral of a red barn. Hay, still heavy from first cutting; blocks for building forts. Secrets of farm life: dead pigs, syringes, beer cans, rusty knives, and spark plugs. On the lawn, women in dresses and lavender powder. Grandma's wig. Grandma's laugh, almost an embarrassed swallow, brilliant and starshine funny. Fresh mowed carpet; fresh painted fence. A daring touch of the electric wire. A dog that peed on the same wire and yelped in fear. Crickets and night sounds. Grandpa's booming laughter.

Later, same place: Boys talk of girls. Girls talk of boys. Grownups talk in serious tones. There's beer and ice in the galvanized horse tank. A softball game and a beefy, drunk older-cousin. Barbed wire rips green jeans. Taste of rust and blood. A yellow, mosquito tank-top. BB guns and old windows. Welts and knots. Small things die. Inside the house: a couch, a television, and cherry pie. Dirty dishes. A long colonial table. Cleanup can wait until morning. Dogs play. Grownups pass on their old stories. Belly full, sweat coated, and bit. Hair mussed and hungry, again. Fold-out couch in the sewing room. Glasses clank. Wake exhausted.

AMPHIBRACH

todd-PART-ridge is an amphibrach
a metrical foot made up of three syllables: unstressed-stressed-unstressed.

spoken in any fashion or manner, it twists my tongue
my name doesn't feel like me

the ancients name us
flowing brook, laughing mouth
sway fir limb, cedar shade
dirt. root. trees
sky-blue-sky
these are names, by the gods!

tension and release grants musical syllable wings
like D-VOR-ak

tonight, a glass of burgundy
a toast from my chalice—chipped pottery:
to my new name
no syllable
no inflection
no words
!

WE BECOME

our mothers
we take our father's cynical eyes
our grandfather's cheerful countenance
grandma's slow surprise
we become their kitchens
and their tractors in the yard
we want to be like them, so we work hard to become
and we grow older
more tired
our bellies lose their fire
we can't stand the view of our gravity-pulled face
our teeth no longer chew
we hold onto smiles from picnics past
breathe the air like until, at last
our children become us
and we become dust

WALKING JOY HARJO HOME

collecting bold truths in denim and beads
under smother of darkness
past a bramble bush sculpture
of Grandpa Geronimo
stories travel like concentric rhythms of a mouth pebble
tossed softly, plunk
eventually dying

melancholy rock dust paths
lumbering chrome ornaments on the highway
art decco chief racing the wind
cast out from Grandmother's lap

VELVET MUD

velvet mud
only elixir to heal a foot,
cut while climbing rusty barbed wire
toward frog ponds;
feet stained with aquavescent
purple-mulberry paint—
diesel smells,
grease-stained pickup truck;
alfalfa and oat salutations

life as a pollywog

JANUARY 24

the story of the day
you were born:
a hot summer day
in a hayfield
in January

your father carried you
in from the hog barn
in a hat made of hearts

a dragonfly from the pond, followed him
into the house with the big brown radio
"It's a girl," the dragonfly whispered
"We will name her after a royal
herb, Rosemary," grandmother declared

Salvia Rosmarinus

after swaddling you in funny papers
from the Press Citizen, some Murphy boy
or Hunter girl,
or Gene somebody ran like a town crier
without a town
to the farmsteads

legend tells of your first words:
"Shoo Fly" (or "SooooWeee")
then you ran
then you jumped
on your old white horse
from behind, bareback
then you galloped away in a flash!

SPIRIT ADVICE

Spirit 1
shake him awake to the wonders of the world, the luxury of freedoms, forgiveness in nature; if he resists, walk him blindfolded to the river bank so he can listen to the hawks in the spiral sky, gently lay his head in the new grass and let him smell the fodder and decay of clean, honest, black soil; remove his blindfold to reveal the mirage of infinite blueness above—this wonder is yours

Spirit 2
sit across from him in a comfortable and cozy tea shop nook and whisper and laugh as the clatter of tea-making and making pastries swirls around us; laugh in our cups with glee—forgiveness is all there is; forgiveness of yourself first, then forgiveness of others, and forgiveness of the universe and the pieces and parts that make it move

Spirit 3
there are people like you, often camouflaged; use the peripheries of your mind's eye to see them, yet you cannot find them by seeking, and they don't find you, indeed, finding those like you is impossible in one lifetime; it takes many lifetimes

Spirit 4
place two fingers to his lips and sing a song of the ancients, ageless and timeless, and implore him—grab hold of the firsts—hold them—embrace them, fight for the feeling of a heart hearing a song for the first time; a shared breath-kiss, laughter, crying, love; the first iridescence of a beetle back ebony rainbow, the smell of bread and flowers, the first soft hug...in a universe of repeating patterns, fractals and reruns, actions and reactions, births and deaths, hold onto firsts and cultivate the child inside

The Great Spirit
words and questions, questions and words; broken, healed, healed, and broken; world upon world; older, younger—there is no time...no reason to speak

SORRY

she tossed the round pendant in a fit of rage.
I found it near the old metal slide, where the kids play
inscribed on the locket:

To be as humble as a waning moon and as grateful as a sunny afternoon when the birds sing the praises of the moment cause they're free...

I weave the silver filigree through my fingers
a hundred years ago...
a drunk says she's sorry, wants you to forget
but sorry without forgiveness is a noose without a neck
once the gift leaves your hand
ten years to life, without the right of correspondence

SHOVEL AND A PRAYER

I wanna drink from a bottle of red wine on the sandy corner of nowhere and watch the girls walk by and feed off their beautiful, youthful energy; but this old town is dying a slow death and the corner scorns this tired romantic vagabond. There's plenty of jobs out here, where everyone leaves, but not the kind of work that feeds a restless soul. I don't care long as I have a safe place to sleep tonight.

On this flat, sandy piece of forlorn prairie you are nobody without wheels and a place to go; nobody without someone around you to call you one of their own; but alone in a crowd sounds better than just alone, and there's nobody left to take me on Springsteen's chrome road of fire. A fantasy replaced with vigilant untruths which echo off the wood paneling and all the beer signs in this tractor-sized town.

Let's find each other and band together like lost boys; like a lost tribe of dreamers ready to hit the road. But it's far easier to travel alone, so we turn up the heat and turn on the television and sit alone in a dark room with an old couch and blanket. We'll meet up on Saturday night and rage with jokes and smokes and tokes and pokes at the wispy fabric that entombs these bloodied and scarred philosophers; and we'll watch our hair turn grey and pretend that poker chips are golden tickets to another life full of everything we missed the first time. But nobody should drink without reason, and being scared ain't reason enough around here.

So, we've two choices:
wake and do the work that finds us
or lie down and sleep with shallow breath
and dig a hole to lay our bodies down

either way it's a shovel and a prayer

SHE SELLS STARS

<u>She</u>
she sells stars and moonbeams in glass jars
believes everything is good
if you believe it's true, you believe in her
she's got two daddy's, no father
sells rainbows and fluffy clouds
says that's the best sex I ever had
rolls her eyes and sells sticks with cotton candy
she polishes stars
while harvesting blue skies
she sells kisses and wishes
butterflies lift her up
but colored paint hides her bruised soul
she keeps trying
that ain't all she sells

<u>He</u>
he sells boxes and pipes full of smoke
army blanket wool
he cuts the trees and brings them home
hangs the kettle on the fire, cooks wild meats
sells her secrets, back to her for a ransom
feel the soft, worn flannel
his musky scent combining pine needles and tobacco
he hides things in a garage
a pencil without eraser
a broken saw
he believes in the reflection he sees
a pool of forgotten oil
gasoline dreams
he dreams of her

POET'S EPITAPH

efflux of the soul
true deserved happiness
find words later
> *May you find granular wonder*
> *in the infinite night*
> *and festival*
> *in the everyday*

in memory

METAPHOR

Smell of creosote in August. Standing, in the middle of that big trestle bridge over the river where we used to float as youth—fearless, sun-browned; enemies imagined. Broken bottle glass. Mussel shells. Bare feet. Mud. The sun sizzles on the iron with splinters like bone-dry, catfish teeth-needles. Arms akimbo, in the middle of that bridge, 60-feet high, and a train is coming. I feel the rails vibrate. I can jump or swim or run like hell.

My cousin with the freckles and a big mouth yells, "Your situation is a metaphor."

LAD

Many's the verse that saved a young lad's life. Star-crossed and stumbling, mumbling at the stars caught twixt the scribe's pen, soft or sharp, and the perfumed stationary of an imaginary lover

This lad is love struck, and obedient to the caller's command. Allemande and sashay, sweaty palms and a racing heart, I pull the notebook from 'neath the pillow—oh, five hundred adjectives for love

      and a rival, always a rival

Pain comes with detachment, after attachment, for it is much easier to love

      from afar

JOIE IS...

a lusty, busty muse
an unspoken thing
> of things that keeps us fighting for life
this inner compass guiding us turn
> by turn
cogs
springs
belts and pulleys universal

enter the address of *joie de vivre*
wrong turn here,
dead-end there

Joie pushes and pulls
promising a horizon always within reach,
never reaching

finally we arrive
the best music you've never heard
> yet to come
the best sex—upstairs in an old building you haven't occupied...
> yet...
the happiest moment—poised
statue of a cat waiting to pounce
the idealized moment:
> tea in the summer garden,
morning

shame is in not picking up the cup
with both hands
savoring and smiling at the cakes
she offers
climbing the creaky stairs
to lie in *flagrante delicto*
a smile on your face

HONEYSUCKLE

I was the honeysuckle, you were the vine
        damn the unsaid words
        that were left behind

by different paths we arrived; same place
        unity in survival
        our saving grace

                you drove that night, I was too young
                the first time

dirt road, south of town
        I remember it well:
        summer sounds, window down

        stars so clear
        backseat of my car
a memory still near

                thirty-years to the day, you passed
I saw starlight in your eyes

I WRITE HOME

narrating how I harvest rage
and shame in embarrassed bushel
baskets, working beside vaporous
shadows of sharecroppers in white
overalls; singing songs of musical
and cultural miscegenation: Senegalese
drum rhythms and Irish famine
ballads, a lilting melody
        all sweat comes from the same great river

I write home
narrating about my unrepairable car
and how my bank account is scorned

bake a pie Mom,
I will bring the great river home to water your feast

Your Son

ANGELS DANCING ON THE HEAD OF A PIN

We stayed awake that first night
        discussing important things
               like angels dancing on the head of a pin

I went home in the morning
jumpin' across hoods of cars
thinking about angels
and pins
how we bared our sacred scars

I called you that next evening
we talked 'til my ear felt sore
'bout jars filled with fireflies
a Chrysalis full of expectations

                eventually, the laughter stopped
                eventually, death
                the rope they gave you handy
                to hang yourself

You left behind an angel pin
        a cherub and a dove
I wore it to your final dance
holy attire for this unholy bard

and a song I wrote, too late:

So, the copper has turned green
and the spaces in between
are filled
with all the things you have seen
I'll bring you red wine
I'll bring you roses...
only god knows
how hard

GREAT THOUGHTS

your message reaches me from the big table where you sit drinking red wine with a friend; discussing great things

I remember the gramophone,
languid in observation
spinning old tunes from wood
and wire; soundtrack for great things—
birds looking in from outside (winter
brambles lean to listen) through the steamy glass
grey sky forms a base layer, under-painting
colors float on its surface—tints
and shades warm with a flushing, heady
red wine...a spätburgunder?

(Charles the Fat brought the variety to Bodensee in 884. Then, sometime in the 13th century, it took root in the Rheingau. Many great thoughts and great draughts have since filled and emptied the wooden cups of almost drunk beggars and bürgermeisters.)

but my cup sits empty, and I can't
reach the window, to look in, to see your lips
moving with great thoughts—lips red and full with the rich, red-violet
blush of the noble rot—
my stool of three short legs, is modest
and humble at this writing, too short
to sit at your table as an equal, but I am happy to think of you now, great
thoughts swirling like woody smoke-rings dancing
around elk horns, gunpowder wisps and ornamental
feathers on the wall—the comfort of chipped earthenware
and a peaty fire; hope of cotton and wool to protect from uncertain
 noises in the night

to think of great things, to give
them letters, to form
and shape words from the mind
to mouth, to give them air and weight in the weightlessness of the
 chasm between done
and doing; said and saying—this place where every
action begins

I yearn for this place

ÇA M'EST ÉGAL

I want to weep–
I will never see this morning, again

for this morning will never hereafter see me as I am
in these moments
for this azure gradient curtain will not surround me
ever again
for these verdant grain fields, leaning toward
their harvest song,
will never repeat
repeat this same song

I recall the things for which I am thankful,
one by one–
I stop at one:
I am the living universe

ironic twist in the skein
ironic living universe: I see the phrase, *c'est la vie*
5 times today
4 more than I should

I reach for my lazy French phrase book;
Ça m'est égal
       c'est la vie
Ça m'est égal

DIG YOUR OWN GRAVE

A farmer friend stopped me on the road today in his rattletrap, rusted two-door Pontiac Sunbird; windows down; arm out the window for one of the first rides of the year. Both of us smiling, coming out of a long period of social quarantine, with spring appearing in all its slow-moving, unfolding glory; hinting at the explosion of life to come. We chatted in the middle of the road; not stopping traffic, for there is none in my small town.

He recounted that an elderly, mutual friend of ours recently lost his dog—a large, old fella some 20-years old. He called the dog his son, as he never had kids. Our friend is frail, old, pushing up into the low hills of octogenarian territory. My farmer friend, who can see those low hills himself, but is still mostly walking the flatland, offered him the use of his shovel; of his muscles to dig a grave. Having dug that same grave I know, while in mourning, a hand on a shoulder, a smile, and the help of another—if even for a couple hours—is magnified 100-fold.

As he started his wheezy engine, he quipped in a loud voice, "Ya know, why ya gotta live each day like it's your last?" he smiled and paused, "Cause one day, you'll be right!" he exclaimed; chortling. I said, "You're right, and the only grave you can't dig is your own!"

I continued along the path with my sweet old girl, Bailey; also treading the flatlands, but she, too, can see those hills. As we often do, we walked through the local cemetery; hundreds of years worth of names, known and unknown to me. It's a small cemetery with two fresh graves uncovered after the Spring thaw. Winter is harder when you're climbing hills.

Nearly all the gravestones in that cemetery face downhill; west toward the setting sun. And I wonder if they chuckle at the metaphor digging your own grave? Almost no one gets that pleasure.

CAN'T GO HOME AGAIN

The air smells like smoke, snakes, spring
and a loamy spice scent they call "You can't go back again…"

Sunday
before Monday's harsh workaday clamor
I am the emperor
laying supine, clay banks
Middle Raccoon River
willow sapling poles fall from the cut-bank
into turbid, rushing water
before the slender yellow rope whips can dangle like a veil
seining the flotsam and jetsam of river trash
trees shedding their old growth

meandering in the wood tick spring
a reticent bleached
deer antler shed
flowers in the wood
dutchman's breeches
comical first blush

ghosts of the ancients
halloo on the hill
if rocks could sing…
providing harmony when the tile starts running
dirty snow melt on fence rows
baritone chorus
contra bass crystalline

redwing blackbirds gather by the creek
fighting over territory
swaying on a scrub tree in the swabbing breeze
they see secrets they can't keep

though you know it's time
memories and places aren't the same

it's true
you can't go home again

COUGHING UP THUNDER

little red-haired girl
playing ukulele with a
wry smile
she pulled it out of me:
laughter–
pulled a bright feather from a
dusty whiskey
bottle

from the belly, like
coughing up thunder

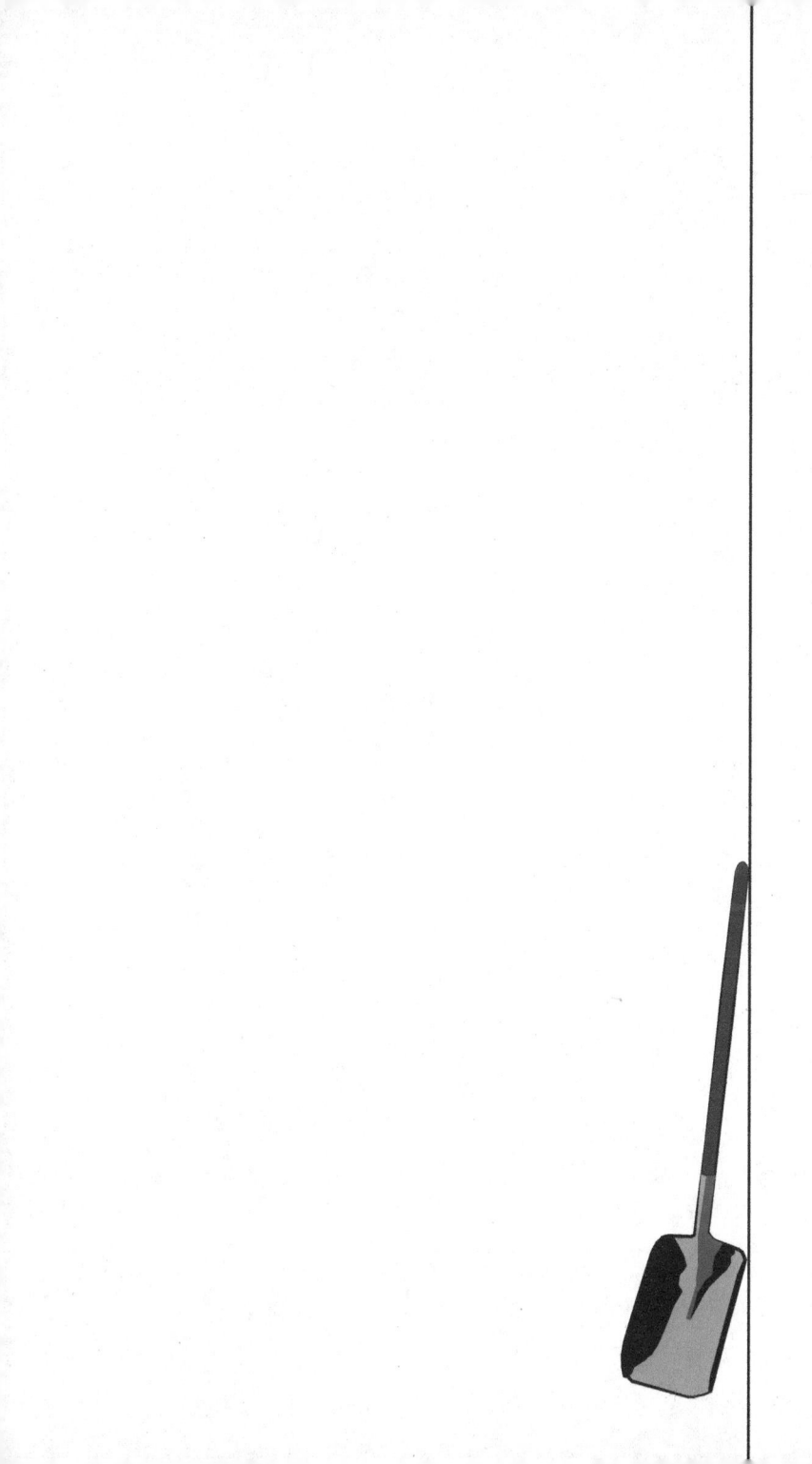

Todd Partridge is a musician, poet and business leader. He has spent most of his life in West-Central Iowa. His music and professional career have taken him all over the U.S. and the world, meeting people and making stories.

www.ingramcontent.com/pod-product-compliance
Lightning Source LLC
Chambersburg PA
CBHW011958090526
44590CB00023B/3778